Walter Lowenfels
Reality Prime
Selected Poems

D1572283

REALITY
PRIME

selected poems

Walter Lowenfels

edited with an introduction by Joel Lewis

Talisman House, Publishers
Jersey City, New Jersey

Published in the United States of America by
Talisman House, Publishers
P.O. Box 3157
Jersey City, New Jersey 07303-3157

Manufactured in the United Sates of America
Printed on acid-free paper

"To Walter Lowenfels" by Tim Dlugos is reprinted with the permission of the estate of Tim Dlugos. Permission to reprint the enclosed selections by Walter Lowenfels was granted by Manna Lowenfels, Literary Executrix for the Estate of Walter Lowenfels; these include "Epistle to C. S. Concerning Burial in Illinois," "From an Exposition of Power and Industrial Machinery," *Apollinaire an Elegy, Elegy in the Manner of a Requiem in Memory of D. H. Lawrence, The Suicide,* "Steel 1937," "Alcoa," "Steel" ("What is it? A Commodity?"), "Steel" ("Steel was something else once in someone's head"), "The Nightingale," "Every Poem Is a Love Poem," "Elegy for the Old Language," "Jukebox in the Coalfields," "Good-Bye, Jargon," "Welcome Home to Cubby," "For a Hemiplegic," "American Voices (2)," "Message from Bert Brecht," "Epitaph for My Punctuation," "R. I. P. (after François Villon)."

Library of Congress Cataloging-in-Publication Data

Lowenfels, Walter, 1897-1976.
    Reality prime : selected poems / Walter Lowenfels ; edited with an
    introduction by Joel Lewis.
        p.   cm.
        ISBN 1-883689-72-4 (alk. paper). — ISBN 1-883689-71-6 (pbk. : alk. paper)
        I. Lewis, Joel. II. Title
    PS3523.O92R37   1998
    811'.52—dc21   98-39219
                                                                     CIP

CONTENTS

"To Walter Lowenfels" by Tim Dlugos . . . 1

Introduction by Joel Lewis . . . 3

Acknowledgments . . . 15

from *Episodes and Epistles* (1925)
    "Epistle to C. S. Concerning Burial in Illinois" . . . 29
    "From an Exposition of Power and Industrial
        Machinery" . . . 22

Apollinaire an Elegy (1930) . . . 25

Elegy in the Manner of a Requiem in Memory of D. H. Lawrence
    (1932) . . . 37

The Suicide (1934) . . . 57

from *Steel 1937* (1938)
    "Steel 1937" . . . 87
    "Alcoa" . . . 89
    "Steel" ("What is it? A Commodity?") . . . 91
    "Steel" ("Steel was something else once in someone's
        head") . . . 92

from *Some Deaths* (1964)
    "The Nightingale" . . . 94
    "Every Poem Is a Love Poem" . . . 96

"Elegy for the Old Language" . . . 98

"Jukebox in the Coalfields" . . . 100

"Good-Bye, Jargon" . . . 101

"Welcome Home to Cubby" . . . 102

"For a Hemiplegic" . . . 103

from *Land of Roseberries* (1965)

"American Voices (2)" . . . 108

from *Translations from Scorpius* (1966)

"Message from Bert Brecht" . . . 111

from *The Portable Walter* (1968)

"Epitaph for My Punctuation" . . . 112

"R. I. P. (after François Villon)" . . . 113

To Walter Lowenfels

by Tim Dlugos

You had four real ones of your own, so why
did you write *To an Imaginary
Daughter?* I found it in the Books
for a Buck bin at Barnes & Noble,
your signature inside, a copy you'd inscribed
to someone whom you'd just rejected
for one of your anthologies of wooly
Movement writing, to which you gave your life
in language of your time, the Great Depression.
It's depressing how unrecognizable
your name's become; with Hemingway and
Henry Miller, one of the three
most prominent and best expatriate
writers in Paris; author of *Steel*,
the pamphlet that made bosses of the day
see Red. Your popularity
like vaunted winds of change, swept through
the corners of the world lit by Left-Lit
and out the window, like the wind today
that drove me into Barnes & Noble.
It's cold out there when no one knows
your name. Spokesman, working-class
Whitmanic bard, poet of the brave
new world, speaker of demotic
democratic truths, mover and shaker, shock-troop
of the Revolution, too-accessible
parent of forgotten books: I know your slim
affected and affecting offspring
only because some miffed, less-than-forgotten
scribbler sold it off for change.

The verdict of the History you used
as engine and excuse is not in yet,
you'd say. I'll stick around.
But I'm haunted by the lack of rhyme
and reason in how power dwindles down
from clarity and massive sweep
of language to a garrulous old man
in Peekskill serving French bread and Bordeaux
to luncheon guests. "He wore a black beret;
the old days were important to him."

Father of vanished texts, where went your truth?
The wind has cleared away your agitprop,
your art, your bromides, your imaginings
of world, or word, or children strong of grip
enough to clasp, to spare your voice.

Introduction

> Poetry has always been a craft for me, a skill with rhythms, nuances, glimmers, colors, shades, parallels: a man at a machine, a die maker at a typewriter, a mason building an edifice in paper.
>
> —Walter Lowenfels

My engagement with Walter Lowenfels began in the late seventies, when, along with a group of poetry cronies, I took to haunting used bookstores in New York and New Jersey in search of poetry "discoveries." One friend encountered Tram Coombs, a now-obscure disciple of William Carlos Williams who wrote homoerotic verse using the doctor's method of the variable foot. I came across *The Portable Walter*, an anthology of Lowenfels' prose and poetry published by International Publishers, the publishing arm of the Communist Party USA. I was befuddled by the faux-psychedelic cover — a weak commie ploy, no doubt, to lure unsuspecting poetry dupes like me. It was a buck, and the work intrigued me, so I bought it.

After that, I collected his work whenever and wherever I could find it. Emerging out of a left-political college world into a scene at The Poetry Project that was often defiantly apolitical, I found Lowenfels' soft-shoe left politics resonated with my own take on things. Unlike the work of many political poets of the Vietnam era, Lowenfels' poetry was rarely angry or rhetorical. His Marxism was closest to that of philosopher Ernst Bloch, who espoused a utopian Marxist vision while remaining a functionary in the East German Communist Party.

The centennial of Lowenfels' birth sparked my desire for a selected poems. All of Lowenfels' books were out of print, and his work was almost unknown to the current generation of young poets. His disappearance from the poetic radar screen can be attributed to several factors. First there are the problematics of the small press world. The poetry pamphlets Lowenfels put out have a "fugitive" aura, reflecting the nature of many small press books before desktop publishing. It was his anthologies of other writers' works, published by mainstream houses such as Vintage, Crown, and Delacorte, that gave Lowenfels visibility. His last works indicate that he was attempting to collect his later poetry, but no such manuscript was found among his literary effects.

Secondly, Lowenfels' obvious political stance did not wear well as the nation veered politically to the right in the years after Vietnam and Watergate. Though an unconventional comrade, referring to his poetry as "socialist surrealist" and attacking Nikita Kruschev in the pages of a Communist journal for his Zhdanovist criticism of modern art, he remained an active Party member up till the time of his death, despite the invasion of Hungary, the revelations of Stalin's atrocities, and the invasion of Czechoslovakia. I would like to believe that Lowenfels maintained his loyalty to Communism for the same reasons as did the great Scot poet Hugh MacDiarmid — to register a protest against world capitalist domination. His late poetry was in fact remarkably low-keyed in its espousal of the Marxist world view. "The goal of life isn't socialism," he wrote in *The Revolution Is To Be Human*; "the goal of socialism is to live. [This] only states the coordinates of the problem. What counts is how a poem is made of it."

Lastly, Lowenfels, who devoted so much time to the work of other poets through his anthologies, appeared to spend less on his own oeuvre. According to his daughter and literary executrix, Manna Lowenfels Perpelitt, Lowenfels was uninterested in revisiting his past and held a certain antipathy toward the poetry of his early years. His greatest achievements as a poet — the "Death Trilogy" of his Paris years — are published together for the first time in the present volume. His version of the Apollinaire elegy in *Some Deaths* cuts that lengthy poem to a few pages. He never reprinted anything from his second volume, *Finale of Seem*, and only reprinted a revised version of "Lullaby for Rosa Luxembourg" from his excellent pamphlet, *Steel 1937* — his last book before fifteen years of poetic silence. During the latter part of his career, he made a major stylistic shift from the surrealist firestorms of his early years. Paralleling William Carlos Williams' explorations in *Paterson*, he began using documentary and found material, including his own substantial correspondence, as a major source for his poetry. He was particularly intrigued with the "anti-poetic" (in Wallace

Stevens' words) language of the scientific and industrial worlds and constructed numerous poems using these materials.

After being given the go-ahead by Ed Foster of Talisman House for a volume of selected poems, I contacted Ms. Perpelitt. A series of phone conversations led to her approval for the project. *Reality Prime* is, I'm happy to report, the most comprehensive overview of Walter Lowenfels' poetry ever published.

Walter Lowenfels was born in New York City on 10 May 1897 into a prosperous German-Jewish family of butter merchants (the company, now Hotel Bar Butter, still exists, although no longer in family hands). As a boy, Lowenfels was an indifferent student, attending schools that specialized in priming wealthy but educationally problematic students for the College Entrance Exams, for which he received "some of the lowest marks ever recorded." College being out of the question, he began working in the family business. World War I intervened, and like many patriotic young men, Lowenfels enlisted but spent his tour of duty entirely on bases in the United States.

After the Armistice, Lowenfels returned to the family business, now a major player in the butterfat world. Around this time he began to write poetry. His first publication, a ballade for Edna St. Vincent Millay, appeared in the Franklin P. Adams ("F. P. A.") Conning Tower column of the *Daily Mail*, which served during the twenties as an important venue for budding writers of light verse. "Epistle to C. S. on Mine Burial in Illinois," about a group of miners killed in a strike who were deprived of proper burial, was his first significant poem. The C. S. to whom the poem was addressed was Carl Sandburg, who wrote to the author, "I know the ashes and tears of all its lines. It is a document and a chant."

Lowenfels' first book, *Episodes and Epistles*, was published in 1925. The one poem in the volume that points to his mature work is "Form and Exposition of Power and Industrial Machinery," whose vocabulary derives entirely from industrial and technical terminologies.

Fairly ignorant, as he would later admit, of the Modernist revolution in America, Lowenfels decided that to become a fully com-- mitted poet, he must follow other voluntary American exiles to Paris.

His father, aghast at the idea of his son leaving the butter business, paid for his European passage in order for him to be analyzed by Sigmund Freud. Lowenfels notes, "I took a slow boat to Spain and never got to Vienna."

Upon his arrival in Paris in 1926, Lowenfels married his fiancée, Lillian Apotheker, the college-educated daughter of a Yiddish scholar and humorist whose pen name was Hinke Dinke Schiemazel ("Limping Ne'er-do-Well"). To support themselves and their eventual family of four daughters, Lillian worked as a fashion correspondent while Lowenfels became an apartment broker, counting among his clients Tristan Tzara, Marc Chagall, and Archibald MacLeish.

Soon Lowenfels was deeply involved in the expatriate arts community of Paris. With his friend Michael Fraenkel, he launched the Anonymous Movement, which advocated total anonymity in the arts. "By remaining anonymous," one nameless manifesto proclaimed, "the artist dedicates to all creation what is most important — his own creative efforts."

Fraenkel and Lowenfels founded Carrefour Press to publish anonymous works, but lack of funds prevented their publishing the anonymous writings of F. Scott Fitzgerald, Michael Arlen, and Samuel Beckett. Lowenfels recalled trying to explain his theories to Beckett, who simply nodded and said nothing. Lowenfels burst into a rage and yelled, "You sit there saying nothing while the world is going to pieces. What do you want? What do you want to do?" Beckett dryly replied: "Walter, all I want to do is sit on my ass and fart and think of Dante."

The Anonymous Movement came to an abrupt end when Lowenfels launched an unsuccessful plagiarism suit against the authors of the play *Of Thee I Sing*, who he claimed had stolen scenes and dialogues from his anonymous play *U.S.A. with Music*. To launch his suit, he had to reveal his own authorship and thus was forced to bring to an end his somewhat quixotic movement.

In 1929, the British house Heinemann published his *Finale of Seem*, a sequence of four long poems that reflect the enormous influence of T. S. Eliot following the publication of "The Waste Land." In 1930, he published the first of three long poems that established his reputation as a major expatriate American poet. *Apollinaire an Elegy* (1930), *Elegy in the Manner of a Requiem in Memory of D. H. Lawrence* (1932), and *The Suicide* (1934) remain almost forgotten minor Modernist masterpieces. With the exception of *Apollinaire*, the poems, referred to collectively by their author as *Some Deaths*, have never been republished in their original versions. The truncated versions Lowenfels published in later books do not convey the energy and tension of the originals, which fuse a slightly formalist rhetoric and form with the oxygen of surrealism to produce amazingly original poems. Kenneth Rexroth, Lowenfels' most ardent supporter, called these poems "impressive works, epoch-making in the evolution of American poetry," and went on to declare, "Lowenfels is thus one of the most significant poets of my generation."

The *Some Deaths* sequence, which the author referred to as "philosophical elegies," reflect Lowenfels' association with Fraenkel, novelist Henry Miller, and the novelist-diarist Anaïs Nin, fellow members of the so-called "death school" of writing (Fraenkel and Miller engaged in a massive correspondence on death, published years later as the "Hamlet" correspondence). The death thematic has its origins in the collapse of world capitalism and the simultaneous rise of fascism. "Death is the moral force of the world," wrote Lowenfels in 1929. Decades later, in 1976, he told Jonathan Cott, "We had the idea the world was dead and that the only thing you could do was to write poems about it."

Death and suicide haunted Lowenfels' work for the rest of his career but were later cast in political, rather than existential, terms. Death and suicide were seen as an integral part of capitalist culture; "to create out of death," as Lowenfels notes in his prose work *The Revolution Is To Be Human*, remained the artist's hope. In a 1964 letter to his sister-in-law Nan Braymer (a co-collaborator on many projects and a close literary adviser), he wrote, "I never gave up my belief in death. Perhaps that's the essential continuity between my years as a poet in Paris, then as a reporter and editor of the *Daily Worker*, and thereafter my return to poems. There was a change, but the essential difference was in locating the source of the petrification and the life growing out of it. My researches finally led me to Hegel and thence to Marx and the discovery that it wasn't 'the world' en tout that was death to the creative process to which I was dedicated, but that layer of the world that dominates the northwestern hemisphere."

Despite his participation in the Miller/Fraenkel conversation on death, Lowenfels was looking elsewhere for answers. "Elsewhere" in the thirties was, more often than not, to be found in the writings of Karl Marx. In 1932 Lowenfels began attending Communist Party rallies at the Salle Bullier on the Boulevard St. Michel. That same year, he wrote to both Miller and Fraenkel, "The insoluble contradictions arising in the social structure are reflected in the personality of the poet. We go to pieces inwardly and, as we sing, toss up brittle pieces of ourselves. And what is it that we have reflected? Nothing more than that Mellon owns all the aluminum in the world and it's killing us."

In November 1934, Lowenfels and his family returned to New York and the family's butter business. A December 1934 profile in the *New York Herald Tribune* catches his transition from idealism to Communism. He discusses his plan for a six-hundred-page poem called *Reality Prime* that would be "an explicit description of the poet's point of view, which is the creative point of view as distinguished from the religious, the philosophic or the scientific." Later in the article, he mentions that "[Louis] Aragon is making Communist poetry at Belleville, the workmen's quarters. All the young men with intelligence enough to be creative are interested in social matters." His brother Albert (known to a generation of New Yorkers as "Al the butter man" in the folksy Hotel Bar butter newspaper ads) was somewhat nonplused by his brother's artistic ambitions. "Oh, I guess he's just a poet in the butter business," he told the reporter. "But Walter's a good butter merchant. Don't forget that."

Lowenfels' poetry pamphlet *Steel 1937* documents his first years back in the United States. The title refers to the drive to unionize "Little Steel" (as the smaller steel producers were called) and, perhaps, obliquely to the Spanish Civil War, two issues of great concern to the CPUSA. Fifty years after its publication, *Steel 1937* remains fascinating for its fusion of the furious style of the *Some Deaths* sequence with

Lowenfels' deepening commitment to Communism. However, compared to the official Communist verse that appeared in *New Masses* during this period (writers such as H. H. Lewis, Sol Furanof, and Kenneth Fearing), Lowenfels' work was far too experimental and surrealist for Party dictates on what was considered poetry for the working class. Perhaps like fellow traveler Carl Rakosi, Lowenfels chose silence rather than write "official" verse; citing his unhappiness with *Steel 1937*, he subsequently withdrew from poetry for almost fifteen years.

By 1938, Lowenfels had left the butter business and settled in Philadelphia. He worked as a reporter, then as an editor, for the Pennsylvania edition of the *Daily Worker*, the CPUSA's official newspaper. His wife Lillian found a position as a schoolteacher in the Philadelphia school system. His comrades and friends of this period (among them composer Earl Robinson, members of the Almanac Singers, and Paul Robeson) knew nothing about his days as a poet in Paris.

On 23 July 1953, at 2:00 a.m., eight FBI agents raided the Lowenfels' family home in May's Landing, New Jersey. As an editor for the *Daily Worker*, Lowenfels was charged with "conspiring to teach and advocate the overthrow of the government by force and violence" under the terms of the Smith Act, which made membership in the CPUSA illegal. Allowed to take one book with him, Lowenfels chose an unabridged edition of Whitman's *Leaves of Grass*. He spent several weeks in jail before his $100,000 bail was reduced to $10,000.

Lowenfels had quietly returned to poetry shortly before his arrest. During his six-month trial, he wrote sonnets and translated Dante and Baudelaire. He was sentenced to two years in prison for violations of the Smith Act, but the conviction was overturned in 1957 due to lack of evidence.

Unfortunately, the Lowenfels family troubles were not at an end. A year after her husband's arrest, Lillian was called up before a House Un-American Activities Committee, which resulted in her being fired from her teaching job in Philadelphia. In 1958, she suffered a stroke that left her a hemiplegic for the remaining seventeen years of her life, during which time she was cared for almost entirely by her husband. Friends of the Lowenfels whom I interviewed for this book spoke vividly of his devotion to his wife and the selfless manner with which he cared for her.

Lowenfels' first poems after his long absence from verse, *The Prisoners* and *Sonnets of Love and Liberty*, suffer somewhat formalistically and mostly reflect the Communist Party ideology of the McCarthy era. The strength of his subsequent work seems to derive from three significant events: (1) Kruschev's revelations of Stalin's crimes in 1956, (2) the emergence of the poetry associated with *The New American Poetry*, and (3) various liberation struggles, both in the Third World and in the South. Unlike many artists who chose to leave by the time of the Hitler-Stalin pact, Lowenfels remained an unapologetic life-member of the Communist Party from the mid-thirties until his death. The reason for this allegiance may well lie in his quasi-mystical, utopian vision, which lacks the cynicism and caustic world view characteristic of the intellectual culture of the Communist movement. His approach is closer to the universalist humanism espoused by his friends Pete Seeger, Earl Robinson, and Lee Hays (with whom he co-wrote the classic song "Wasn't That a Time") and by the folk music community before its commercialization in the late fifties. Compared to political poets like Amiri Baraka, June Jordan, and James Scully, Lowenfels' work, usually written in the middle voice, is gentle. His reliance on found materials in his late work often places the notion of authorial presence under question and revisits his early Anonymous Movement inspiration.

In the early sixties, Lowenfels moved to Peekskill, New York. In 1964, *Some Deaths*, a selection of his poems published by Jargon Press at the urging of Louis Zukofsky and Kenneth Rexroth, brought him into contact with writers as diverse as Allen Ginsberg, Howard McCord, Nancy Willard, Clarence Major, Ishmael Reed, Armand Schwerner, and Dick Lourie. The work also introduced Lowenfels to the non-mainstream poetry audience of the period. At a time when many poets were seeking out forgotten poets like Mina Loy or searching rare book collections for Williams' experimental texts from the twenties, Lowenfels must have been a revelation — an ex-Parisian exile who was hip to the modern world and not shackled to his past. Allen Ginsberg praised the revised version of "The Suicide," declaring, ". . . your old man sincerity at the end is beautiful — the wilder you get in poetry the better I like it and I am amazed by your intelligence." Lowenfels became a familiar figure at the Cafe Metro and later at The Poetry Project at St. Mark's. Although not the best of readers, he would often perform with musical accompaniment by artists such as clarinetist Perry Robinson, son of his friend Earl Robinson.

Around the same time, Lowenfels embarked on his career as an anthologist. He edited two popular selections from Whitman's writings as well as the very well received *Poets of Today* anthology. Another anthology, *Where Is Vietnam?*, became a virtual bible for many in the antiwar movement.

If Lowenfels is remembered at all today, it is largely due to these widely distributed anthologies. While they clearly served as a primary source of income, Lowenfels also felt they were central to his oeuvre. In 1966, he told interviewers Jack Lindeman and Richard O'Connell:

> Jack [Lindeman] writes that what counts is my poetry. But I'm concerned with the totality of what I'm doing. To exclude my anthologies is to miss that total creative impact. They're not my words, they're the other guys' words, but I'm making a collage of poems. I am not doing anthologies the way other people do anthologies for schools, literary purposes, academic purposes and so forth. Each one of my anthologies is a creative conception.

The collective ideological thrust that unifies the anthologies is Lowenfels' opposition to what he dubbed "the white poetry syndicate." The collections include raw poets like Charles Bukowski and Ray Bremser and hip black poets like Ray Durem and Calvin Herton. Lowenfels' goal was nothing less than to dissolve the Western notion of "literature," reclaim poetry from those who had made it "a pedant's game" (in Basil Bunting's trenchant phrase), and replace it with a "writing life where there is no difference between poem and non-poem, verse and prose, letter and elegy."

Lowenfels' late work owes much to William Carlos Williams (particularly the long poem *Paterson*) and the Turkish Communist poet Nazim Hikmet. Although Lowenfels had met Williams in Paris, he had not paid attention to his work until his return to poetry three decades later. In the poetry stacks of Philadelphia's Logan Square library, he discovered *Paterson*:

> This was a revelation to me; here he had been writing all along, making inventions in rhythms, using documentary material, newspaper quotes, combining prose letters with verse, and I hadn't known anything about it, although on my own I had come to somewhat parallel discoveries.

Hikmet, too, had used documentary materials, but, more important, he was a committed (and much imprisoned) Communist writer who managed to retain the creative impulses of Mayakovsky without bending to the dictates of the Zhdanovist Social Realist aesthetic.

Lowenfels' final years were taken up with prose projects that unfortunately remain for the most part unpublished. Only one section of his massive autobiography, *My Many Lives*, made it into print, in a very limited edition. A habitual letter writer, Lowenfels also put together a volume of correspondence (his letters form the core of many of his prose works). Sadly, what Lowenfels, his friends, and his family consider his magnum opus — *The Autobiography of an Empire*, a massive documentary history of the United States as told through visual materials, letters, and documents — remains somewhere in manuscript among the dozens of unsorted boxes of his papers in Yale University's Beineke library. At one point it was to be published by Stonehill Press, with an introduction by Angela Davis, but the press went out of business before the work could be printed.

Two books that did find a publisher, *To an Imaginary Daughter* and *The Revolution Is To Be Human*, stand as the great accomplishments of his last years. Prose works that defy precise categorization, both are subtle meditations on art, life, and politics, three areas Lowenfels believed were inherently interconnected. The books have a casual, introspective quality. In a letter to the English poet Cressida Lindsay, Lowenfels states, "Letters (*To An Imaginary Daughter*) aren't 'written' like books. They are happenings when everything else including the typewriter is lost, and there's nothing to say except what always escapes and only later turns out to be the important thing."

Lowenfels died on 7 July 1976 after a long struggle with cancer. Though many of his projects were unfinished, he remained active almost until the end. His last anthology project, *For Neruda, for Chile*, offers a collective poetic voice of protest against the brutal military dictatorship that overthrew the democratically elected Allende presidency. At a memorial held in October 1976, Ruby Dee, Ossie Davis, Pete Seeger, Nancy Willard, and Herbert Aptheker were among many who spoke in tribute to his remarkable life.

What significance does Lowenfels' poetry hold for us at the end of the twentieth century? The Soviet Communism he so ardently supported has all but evaporated, and no organized opposition to a world capitalist system has arisen in its place. For those opposed to "the creeping meatball" (Abbie Hoffman's colorful equivalent for "the ruling class"), no haven like "The Movement," about which Lowenfels so lovingly wrote, exists.

Still, although the "white poetry syndicate" has not exactly vanished, it certainly lacks the power it wielded back in the days when Robert Lowell & Co. were cartographers of the American poetry map. Anthologies such as Paul Hoover's selection of post-modern poetry and the two-volume Rothenberg/Joris *Poetry for the Millennium* would never have found a publisher fifteen years ago. Poetry, in some ineffable and hard-to-quantify manner, has become a popular, if marginal, activity. And dozens of young writers have emerged in a digitalized era to take up the most Luddite of the arts.

Lowenfels understood poetry as a form of resistance. "The poem is an effort today," he noted, "along with all others, to defend the integrity and dignity of human personality against the world's statistical claw." But he also understood that negating this resistance is the underlying sentimentality and nostalgia which haunts works that borrow the conventions of the past:

My campaign against nostalgia has its base in language, i.e., to use the language of today for today's emotions: the clean, new scientific word, woven into the fabric of the poem so quietly the reader doesn't sense anything but the contemporary pulse modulation. That's the test of language — that it is alive with today's electronics — not Ben Franklin's kite key.

(The Revolution Is To Be Human, p. 21)

I believe that the time is ripe for Lowenfels' particular blend of humanistic vision and social politics and that Lowenfels' work will establish itself as a major rediscovery in twentieth-century American poetry. From the pyrotechnics of his Paris verse to the "scientific surrealism" of his last works, Lowenfels is always "on the job," trying to figure out the "mess" that seems to be the nameless, uncarved block here in Cash Nexus, USA. "We are not in danger of poems dying out," Lowenfels wrote to Jonathan Williams in 1959; "the danger is that something that passes for poems will get embalmed in certain university courses while the Literary Underground keeps the real current going. . . . For anyone to have poems anytime somebody has to live poems all the time. . . ."

Joel Lewis
8.11.98
Hoboken, NJ

Acknowledgments

My greatest thanks goes to Manna Lowenfels-Perpelitt, one of Walter Lowenfels' four daughters and the executrix of his estate. She gave me permission to assemble a volume of his selected poems and made available her knowledge of her father's work (a fine poet, she worked closely with him during the last decade of his life) together with materials that were invaluable in the preparation of this volume. I hope this collection does justice to her father's work and restores him to the prominence he deserves.

A tip o' the hat, again, to Talisman House publisher Ed Foster. After suffering my callow young poet self, he recovered enough trust in me to consent to this project and my collection of Ted Berrigan's talks. For his amazing skills as an editor, poet and person, I can only pay him the highest compliment of my childhood: "Gee, I wish that Ed were Jewish!"

To thank Talisman is also, and especially, to thank Zoë English — an editor's editor, who is also a terrific person.

My wife, Sandy Flitterman-Lewis, is the invisible redactor of much of my prose — a combination of her wise ways and my unstable grammatical skills. Our ongoing fourteen-year conversation and her continual support of even my most scatter-brained ideas is the quotidian alchemy that allows me to dream dreams.

Special thanks to Jonathan Cott's profile of Walter Lowenfels (in his book of interviews, *Forever Young* (New York: Random House, 1977), an invaluable source of information on the poet.

Further kudos to Gary Lenhart, Armand Schwerner, Gus Hall, Dan Georgakas, Ed Friedman, the staff at the New York Public Library, Patricia Willis of the Beineke Library, Amiri Baraka, the Buffalo Poetics List, Ibex and Emo Bumpás, Chris Strofollino, and others for their advice, talk and encouragement.

A special thanks to my early day poetry cronies — Ed Smith and Mike Reardon, two-thirds of our Nungesser Poets affinity group.

Remembering day-long bookstore binges, Rutt's Hut hotdogs and round-robin readings atop the Hudson Palisades.

Reality Prime

Epistle to C. S. Concerning Burial in Illinois

Herrin is a long way from here
and there are piles of unknown dead in Potter's Field;
but there is something about being buried in dark, coal ground
    with a June sun roaring and blazing overhead,
        and nobody around to say: "Yeah, he was a hard workin' feller, and
        sent money home regular."

There are sixteen of them on Herrin Hill
    and I'll bet they were good huskies —
Lithuanians, Swedes, Poles, Czechs. . . .
You've seen them loafing over the rail of an ocean liner —
    bulging, hairy arms, and thick faces. . . .

Melt them into Americans in a coal mine . . .
Eight on and eight off and every other Sunday . . .
Sunday, with stiff clothes,
    hanging around the corner, or playing billiards in the pool parlor.
. . . 20 lira to the dollar and an Olive Patch near Florence some day . . .
    (olive trees near Florence are gray silver in the sun!)

They don't understand Union language;
But even a Swede can hear a bullet talk . . .
Round 'em up . . . corral 'em at the edge of town . . . and give 'em the gat.
The earth in Herrin is ground with coal dust and murky cinders
    And a couple of quarts of blood.
Front pages, a grand jury, and sixteen unidentified bodies in the Town
        Hall.
If no one shows up, bury 'em on Thursday, boys.

A little, stark line winds out of town and up Herrin Hill,
and it's hot as Hell in the sun.
It doesn't take many to bury sixteen —
a few body carriers, a union inspector, a preacher;
and the A. P. Man —

> ". . . unidentified dead were given a simple burial to-day by the
> union officials . . . they committed their
> bodies to earth but forgot to give their
> souls to God . . ."

It makes me nervous . . . those sixteen wingless souls, floundering and
      flopping around, six feet under Hell.

They buried themselves that day:
One cubic inch out of the liver and guts of
      128,000,000 folks in the U. S. A., and
      987,000,000 in China, Peru, and points east
is buried forever, six feet under the top of Herrin Hill . . .
Also:
      1 patch of gray silver that was an Olive Grove near Florence;
      2 fishing smacks off the coast of Naples, heavy with a good catch;
      4 small acre farms in Poland.
      and a half dozen, or so, new starts in Nebraska Wyoming and
         California.
I'm going to organize a bugle blowing, prayer meeting for 16 dead
      huskies . . .
Come on, you bartenders,
      lunch roomers,
      billiard parlorites,
      whores,
      etcetera.
Come on, all you casuals who knew them —
We're going to have a brass band prayer meeting
      and let out a prayer that will bust clean through
      and shiver down in Hell

and stop the worms a minute. . . .
A prayer that will break away from the flat-faced glare of the sun
and reach cool darkness. . . .
And if there is Anyone listening beyond the hills . . .
and if . . . and if . . .
>   (and of all "and ifs" that is the most sullen desperate),
>   Let Him sprout wings
>   on dry, meat-picked bopes
>   and give them a sail to Heaven.

From an Exposition of Power and Industrial Machinery[*]

    unit aligning power transmission
    non return vertical indicator
    pump governing nose
    return trap compensating joint
    expanding lathe mandrel

    make up water
    boiler blow down
    bleach liquor
    stream flow
    glass steam trap
    air cooled wall for powdered coal

    forged steel header
    tongue and groove joint with copper
        gaskets, welded flanges
    multiple retort underfeed stoker
    balanced seatless blow-off valve
    spur gear speed transformer
    multiwhirl baffle
    bleeder turbine

    Open float inspirator and injector
    steam jet air pump
    super simplex pulverizer
    gyrating cruster

---

[*] This list records some names of machines and machine parts. I have arranged this particular sequence but the words are the exact engineering terminology.

crushing chamber
armature spider
diamond valve head
stoker fired boiler
adjusted spray nozzle
blending turbine
reciprocating boiler feed
oil firing front natural draft

forged steel filings and unions
sylphon fuel oil interlocking
quick change chuck and collet
weightometer
safety water columns
seamless copper float
screw anchor
float chamber
exhaust relief valve
reverse current valve
self sealing evaporator

clipper belt lacer
flexible coupling
no contact indicator
tandem blow off
hanger boxes
pillar boxes
drop forged steel body
hardened worms with thread ground
caustic soda ash
cement slurry metallurgical slimes

carbon steel hand taps
precision high speed ground thread taps
two and three fluted taps
spiral pointed serial hard machine screw

> bent shank tapper taps
> mud or washout spindle staybolt
>> coupling taps for pipes and tubes

> short die hobs
> long die hobs for the man who makes his own dies.

Apollinaire an Elegy

It is enough that the night
is full of rain and chimes and angels
like a Spanish cathedral
        with the street
an escala d'oro
the stars descend.

        Forgive the word O Builder
                the poem was between the rain and
                                the chimes
        not in the word but in the angels.

Yours O Apollinaire was an act.
Your name has the sound of a statue
or a temple the eyes have not seen.

        The columns of Baalbek crumble
                architecture remains
        like a dream of the world.

        Building is a vista or a vision
        a spirit that inhabits stone or air
        the persistent soul of objects
        making any everything
        a womb of possibilities.

And green is green!
        And cream is cabbages
                        and red are carrots.
How lovelier than Miss Universe
to live on vegetables and colour that make

each truck lumbering through the rain
a chariot of the Lord.
Lamp posts are golden with the eyes of God
and Apollo drives the horses of the sun
down the street to collect loud garbage

    a thousand departures
for the thousand poems in the mind
and
                    at Burgos
                        the hill

where the Cid persists in grass-eaten stone
    goats ranging the ruined battlements
the mangy couple
making a palace of the broken moat

                      O Spring
still Spring
          forever Spring

    white violets growing there

still blooming wild

           creating still
the mind's persisting Spring.

    And why the oppression of weeping without weeping
    at the emigrants qui
    emplissent de leur odeur le hall de la Gare St-Lazare?
    There is also a theology of gas mains.

    Good-bye
        far away
            good-bye.

There shall be songs of the Argentine

      but in the other sense
you lie still.

We can give you nothing
but what we take
           there's
the cold comfort of objective immortality.
No more the burial with flints.
The witch doctors have gone
              with them
the obscure hopes of earlier Christs.
No more the white bird rises invisibly
to carry the soul from sight.
              For us
the purity of extinction.
Not even Mr. Ford shall lie
with a thousand piston rings
to feed his soul in heaven.

Statistics rule a million millions
the oppression of whose certain numbers
leaves their dying epic as an almanac
and no sadder than the census of East St. Louis.
Tragedy is one
      and one is a poet.

Mort à Guillaume! Mort à Guillaume!
In the street
        below
the mob were shouting
for another William.

It was Armistice Day. The war was over.
In the room a known soldier died.

One voice said *Il l'a coupé.*
From the street
                    the crowds
shouting *Mort à Guillaume.*

This grave stands for no millions.
Here no strangers lay wreaths.
Here no light burns eternally but our own.

His Arc de Triomphe is a structure of the world
not in the word but in the angels
and every taxi horn of Paris
keeps his flame eternally rekindled
not in the sound but in the angels.

His is a continual creation
leading yesterday into tomorrow
making every poem that is a poem
a monument wherein his flame
lights outward the world's plasticity
not toward the word but toward the angels.

It is possibilities
whose unfulfilled passing
obey the laws of tragedy.
                    For mourning
dying is not enough.
There is a logic of death.

We'll visit the graves of all who died too young
to mourn for what we might have known.

This shall be one-soul's day
building its own sorrow
into the gaping body of the earth.

Other deaths
　　　　for other theologies.

This day we mourn this man
because the world
　　　　　　and our world
is less one possibility
still unlisted
in the tables of insured certainty.

We sold liberty bonds in Little Rock, Ark.
We were betrayed on the Russian Front.

Leave us brother
we lived only for this.
We are the dead and the alive.
We enjoyed the smell of being one of many.
We lived for that
and thus for this.
We overcame our destiny and remained
the human race.
We are the millions of heros
　　　　　　we lie here as heros do.
We do no know
the tragedy of peace.
Only we know
our dying was a formality
　　　not an event.

Leave us brother
　　　leave us our war
we *lived* in that
and thus
for this.

　　　Rot his bones
　　　　　　scatter his flesh

he wants nothing from death
but death.
It will not fail him that.

O astronomer move out our stars
light us more light years
                              say
what we see from Mt. Wilson
is Mt. Wilson and heaven and us
        more heaven on earth than there's in heaven
but from my nose
take away this dead fish
of the immortality of the soul.
And O Cholera blight this cult
who make death a fetish
worn in the lapel
like a rotten rose
    who see adventure in extinction
sensation in futility
excitement in worms
        who seek death to live.

This is his purgatory
                    and ours
            a later Christ and the Kingdom
                          within
burning its own ashes by its own flame:
Phœnix
            alive:
dead
        dead.

O Few

        O Poets

                mourn for Apollinaire.

He has sunk and will not rise
                              and still
        through the rainy nights of Paris
moves his unuttered poem
                              and lives
still lives in the mind's persisting Spring.

        He leaves dead death
to be a later revelation of the world
        he mounts into the rain
                              into the night
not like Lycidas into the darkened heavens
but in the moving glitters of the street
he shines a later and lost star.

Weep for the untraced interstellar spaces of a wet pavement.
Weep weep astronomers for a lost poem a lost world.
Weep for you will dot infinity with nebulae
and leave forever unrecorded
the infinity that surrounds the passing footfall
that might have been a diapason of angels
in the singing kingdom of Apollinaire.

Each man to his own dead
and grief that returns with the revolving year
but this death is more than death
        the earth is truly wet with rainy eyes
the world is mourning the world's own death
dying in its own creation in Apollinaire.

Weep weep O world. . . . .
                              I am silent in this sorrow.
This is a service of the rain
                              and the muffled drum of a footfall
and the chimes
                              and the angels.

The city shrivels into darkness
facing a black stone desert toward the day.
A dearth of angels
                              warps the hours
that curl back into clocks
while Time waits in a coma for the sun.
A dearth of angels
                              strips the city to gutters
        and
walls the night
        blackness in blackness
                                    stone in stone
        and
leaves a heart beat and a heart beat
strangers to the world company for me.
A dearth of angels
                              drifts down like a parachute
onto the brain
                        and leaves
it shrouded in its bleakness
and the world in its
        the world to the world and me to me.
A dearth of angels
                        and
the dirge disintegrates to one and one and
                                    one and one
                less
the illuminating analysis of a conjunction . . .

Not the word breaks
but the thought
    not the tongue decomposes
but the brain
    not that thinking is too much
but the mind goes wormy . . . . .

O Anathema
on those shrivelers of the earth
        leaving it beyond seed
a dried bean on a withered stalk
firelessly baked into tasteless hard-tack.

Better the revulsion of worm-white meat
        the activity of disgust
than your drab slab
of inexistence
        seeing fresh pulp
as old tar
        losing the ecstasy of disaster
for a dry doom.

How meagre for company
        whose despair is a wisp of hollow straw
trickling a thin dribble of death
        starvation diet for a flea.
Better be a care-free louse
than a bloodless shell
                        displaying
the appurtenances of a crab
        without claws
        without meat
        without motion
(gone even is the vestige of a sideway scuttle).

How puny your sorrows
        an itching pimple
        irritation of a scab
        sadness of a skin disease
escaping the tragedy of resistance
in an ointment of quick despair
        (sometime
warbling bad sweetness

like an automatic violin
    in a glass case
responding to the nip of any nickel).

Here is something deserted on a beach
lost between a picnic and an ocean
bleached from the slight contact
of too much too little
losing even the last faint odour
    in a last aridity.

O false shell
        false suffering
crying the name for the deed
how tenacious is your brittleness
glazed to a fake eternity
    a dump of hair pins
        corset covers   old cans
(past this wasted frontier
deep is the green country
full of bark and pines).

Better be fungus
        and dot
the dark hollow places
the spaces between roots
and give at least a plop
as you squash out
    when stepped on.

I have seen the trains stand still moving
while I move out standing still.
Toward thee O death are all my journeys
    but the mind bends toward an eye
        that lives in a lamp post

and lights this night
with an x to mark the spot
of its constantly moving horizon.

. . . . . in North Dakota
the night-rising ducks
      over the mounds
      blocking the moon
      burning out
still
      blooming wild
in the mind's persisting Spring.

    O Brain!
in thinking itself there's an excellence of act
that makes a sacrament of processes.

Yours Apollinaire was an act.
Yours is moving world my mind has rested in.
I do not weep at the Gare St-Lazare
but I am moved when I move with you
through the millions in this building
    into building
away from the stale odour of a million nouns
(even now they sleep the sleep of the righteous
while the sparrows are beginning
to look for crumbs and chant Laus Deo
like a choir of early acolytes
chirping in a new day).

    To you
for saving a night
for having been
        for being
throughout the drizzling dark
a priest and a prophet

saying while you say the Seine is there
pointing out pointing out the Eiffel Tower there
that poetry is this and that
            living
                  there.

You who were Provence to those who went before
came into being again
to be Apollinaire to us
            showing to those who saw
                              those who see
a way to build

      making your going out
a coming in

      saying
that death that is the act
is a passing at the point of a possible beginning
making anywhere a beginning
any point a possibility

saying
the world is constantly building
dying into beginning
      saying
the world is enough
and that is enough.

Elegy in the Manner of a Requiem
in Memory of D. H. Lawrence

(Note: This elegy consists of lines 4678 to 5185 from Book II of *Realty Prime*. It is intended for a choral service, in the manner of a Requiem for a dead man. These marginal abbreviations are used: *B*, Baritone; *C*, Chorus; *Q*, Choir; *T*, Tenor; *S*, Soprano; *A*, Contralto; *O*, Bass. The voice directions are approximate, and I have not indicated them throughout. I have had in mind a form of operatic poem: verse, music, moving design, synchronized on a recording instrument: reproduced, from records, privately by the "reader" —W.L.).

In the Valley of the Corpses

T   Phoenicians
            sailors from Tyre
      ghosts of ships that haunt these ports
      you who sought death in strange lands
      among the people of the forest and on northern shores
      here is another whose spirit
      moves through slow afternoons of Riviera chatter
            and Roman teas
      a spirit of familiar death in odd places
      walking newly among the villas and the flowers
            and through the chips.

            Miles centuries days
      from the heart's land I carry his awkward bow
      like a wedding of despair. What else
      out of the wretchedness of one more star ?

C   A polecat alone at night
            the gleam out of the carcass
      a blood spore one tenth in books
      a something we grew with
      like a habit but with an almond taste?

Q 　　　　　　*Hoofed O Phœnix? Wading like a bull*
　　　　　　　　　　　　deep in the hill glades
　　　　　　　the clay faces in the unfooted shadows?

O Winter in the cones
under the rivers under the pines
　　　from the blinded needles
what rituals of what seasons?

out of outward cycles
of rise and fall by rote
an outworn tale of histories
a nursery round of acts and habits
enforced by furniture or climate or this
　　　that looks like death.
It eats among the maggots. And there I beg you
grubs an issue of your grace.

C 　　　*It is better in this*
　　　　not to hear nor to see

B 　　Crossing and recrossing
I killed my eyes and ears

with something like my life
like a blow torch at the back
seeking an elegy for him
dead as the crow flies
dead as the carrion flies
dead as these last rotting roots
in this Atlantis of the mind.

C   *Burn burn . . . . .*
                     and crack brain crack

O   . . . between the ripples
               along the small canals at night
               the voices mirrored in the dark
                     like bright circles in the waters

C   We cannot sink. We cannot rise.
   We freeze. We crack
       to any single thing.

    There is no pain
               only
    a shadow sweeps us
    like a wing above our rock
    to an immolation we do not know.

    We are the human image of the thing
    past the even tide of being
    cast in fossils in the flesh
       and we evade
    the evocation of an instant.

O   And this I call the soul
       doomed to a fastness it cannot know
   but it breaks in splinters to the eye
   without the living eye to hold the whole.

C   We are the should be's of the dead
   doomed to winter it among the squids
   fixed in snows of unaspiring centuries
   in the ice-age of our make-believe
   to freeze through cracks to coalescence
   not to burn the oneness of the thing.

Nor tell a brother we do not know.

Pity us
        torn by stags
who never saw Dionysus in the flesh.

        We perish
without time
                through the long sleeping
without death
                to other spring.

An Acteon who saw
        devoured
not consumed. Too human.
He rots of out corruption.

Q   *O crime! Doubly dead*

        Purifier!
Destroyer! Avenger!
How call you?
grub among the scavengers
Zagreus of the spirit
        of the flesh:

among the corpuscles
between the insects and the angels
gnawing at the edge of things
until the world breaks through
weave O worm a seed you cannot weave
to sprout the world with flowering teeth
to lie with Callisto in the blood
to burn among the riders and the heaven-borne.

In the Valley of the Poet

This is the valley of the sea-spores
and the rain of dead things drop
to lay on the sea-bottom
their eternal floor.
There is no count of centuries
where it has been dark so long
and no seasons change
into day or night
and the tides lay still
in the cold that does not freeze
and a gleam of phosphorescence
that a deep sea thing discloses
before the corridor of the sea's
darkness closes.
    Only here one rises
like a warmer current through the cold
when the darkness closes.

And one

Once the heart rose
like Elijah on a jewel.
I followed it never to return.

And another

 On the stage
a spot light of soliloquy
  lit a halo
the darkness of the outer action
a circus of movement
of division of interruption

of such invisible complication
only the butter is
fruity as a golden guinea
banked to the brim in spruce white tubs
bored with silver sabres
tasted on the blade
and bought and sold.

And another

My time was like an accordion
        stretching out
between each visit
of successive taps upon the door.
I aged three score and ten
too quickly between each shake of the tongue
for others to know
coming and going
how often I died
to compose another me.
By continual suicide
I escaped being similar to myself
which is
            I lived
too slowly
the something else that was always me.

And another

I showed to others
the skeleton only
of what the poem had eaten away.

I was faithless to the rest.
So it went by powder and by crystal
a flame of egophagy

purifying to nothing
    but the ash.
And who'll live by this
    distillation
of secret juices
of small arteries
and for whom
O Jesus of the woods?

Only now three paces away
I see it
and swear by what's between us
all I say is false.
I lived between twos
like a gulley down a valley.
I was also on each hill top.

And so I was three
a magic number
curing snake bite and stings
but not truth
    like the wizard's shirt
full of other color.

I have tolled down the hills
in the tall grass
in the spring.
I have fallen in the waters
in the spring.

    Now was the voice that had opened in the dark
withdrawn and I was left alone
outside a row of cells
a prisoner in a corridor
free behind a row of doors.

This I call the soul
locked from sight
free in a fastness it cannot know.
And for this one lives
and for whom
O Orpheus of the pines?

Rising I rose
a chrysalis into change
and left one drop of blood behind
from the living heights
dropping to the sea floor.

I heard a nightingale among the whales
clean as a shark tooth among the shoals.
It was singing calling
among the sea mammals among the ghouls
the octuples among the souls:

My brother rests among the butter
but something on the wing recalls the ears
when it is south east over Montauk.
There the wind trolls slowly.
But Clambert moves among the climate
moves among the weeds among the blue bells
moves among the hills where the dialect
changes with the ridges
and Clambert changes with the climate.

There is frost among the dew.
On the edges of the spider cases
the tarantula nip their mandibles
among the flies among the beetles
the ocean quells
below the tills below the sea ripples

among the rock shelves the eels
that coil and recoil in hypnotic spells
feasting on crustacea the gravel dribbles.

He moves among the miles
like Switzerland among the blue bells.
But the edelweiss we picked
persists among the leaves.
It is turned to day by day.
It yellows slowly. It spreads its wings.
It folds and unfolds.

There was sun among the hills
among the bells among the fine frost.
Ipakak is also a flower that grows.
Ipakak is a name above the mountains.

The trellisses are made of gold
and the seconds stretch into grills.
Among the butter
an hour was worked into a blossom
on one hand golden on the other
an edelweiss a blue bell or an hour.
It goes stitch by stitch by tower
a poem monumental as a butler
O children that knit their acts
among the butter.

And another

Now is the land seasonal again.
The darkness descends among the moles
and the water below the rocks.
There are in me such tales of flowers and change
of occupation of breathing things

of absorption centrally
I have to look but an instant
to sponge-in living things
to make of any stir a life of tides.
        I call it hawkweed
along the edges of the stone.
It rises like Clambert among the dead.
It sings like Mozart among the buds
of weeks of days of seasons on end
among the walkers and riders and the heaven-borne.

Among the Luminals

So I fled into the thing for him
north with a lash

past your frozen Jesus
your Orpheus in abbatoir

        remember me apostles!

north beyond the fathers
dropping among the cycles
the sweat of pearls among the ices.
Caught trapped
without a word among the luminals?
O Master what rituals of what seasons?

Frozen as the winds blow
above the sky below the roots
among the needles and the cones
an elegy of untranslation
excellent among the trees

high among the sea fauna
and the weeds that wave
among the corals and the shoals.

So I bled into a melt
above the blades above the wrecks
a plankton along the reefs
a stir among the muscles
above the Morris-dancing of the Islanders
among the movers and the ridden
        and the heaven-borne.

Forgive us sea-petals
and remember us not
        as you will not
lipped by the wave
sea-moulded among the waxes.
The straw is in the wind
running like an idiot with moss in the ears.

        What nightmare of the time?
island universes
        dark with exotic blooms
over quicksilver streams
vanishing at the touch?
or this hysteria of others?
moving like the desert locusts in the spring
to the first lake
into death by water
        from drought.

                O parched O thirsting
take lime
        bathe among the heather
be brilliant among the juices.

Build thee less stately mansions
in the groves among the oranges
and forget the visions
for long life among the turtles.

So I made the poem
and otherwise lay chained with others
doomed to ever-lasting dungeons
among the tattered and the torn
writhing below the spires
in the cells below the fastness
staked to the dankness of the soil
devising plans for killing rats
for evading stenches
        and seeping poisons
and stabbing for the heart
to sustain a brother
        in the flesh
blood-drinking
        swimming with Athena
west of Andromeda
        O spires O temples

So your human yolk
flowers like a crab with anemone
only inwardly like the crystal of a cancer
and cracks in the shell
for not being born.

But it acts like a loving thing
like a living thing
                        like an angel
full of good habits.
                        And this
I was too much my cousin
        lay by myself

bred only white mice
        all my dreams
one length of Asia less familiar
and there across the continents
the sperm of the mind
struck from its roots
fertilized monstrosities
        among the vacuums.

And this is the service!
Fouled in the penis
a penitentiary of too closeness
cursed and soaring
                        among the centuries
        among the vectors
among the walkers and the riders and the heaven-borne.

The Return.

C   Dion is dead.
We cannot rise. He cannot sink.

        He is the last
none left to carry a choir of song
to sing a last melody

        O Mute!
Autumn! O master a thousand years away
        lift this dying
into the elegy we missed. Carry this last
        unconquerable
into a harmony we cannot sound . . .
bored with death
tired of dying
in too many places.

B   Autumn! O afterbirth!
     O living death!
     No elegies but estimates
     cold with uncertainties
     conviction
                 one pebble or another.

C   Lord!
           what Lord?
     avenge our slaughtered selves.
     We cannot sink.
     We are sick.
     We are dribbling into death
     and the mind's a quack
             curing nothing with quicksilver.

Q   Hoof-glitterer! Charger in the sun! From the hilltop
     pawing the cliffs and the wild . . .
                       O silver-white
     among the ashes and the constellations
     from the cinders of the seasons
                   sprout

T   Nameless of the other flame!
     Star! Tearless! O heart
             pity this
     monument to elegies?
     a winged victory
        full of a wild enchantment?

A   of how many fathoms-forgotten spring?
     Deeper it lies than the snows.
     Under the sea-bottoms under the dripping sea-dead
     under the dooms in the darkness
     of unchange it lies. It will not thaw.
     It will not move. It will not flood the islands

or any shore. It stays with tomorrow's ghost
in the flower beyond snow.

To Dion

O   Of our aspirations
                    what's to be said
    but that like our buildings and towers
    they were sometimes far-reaching?

B   In eternity we do not meet.
    In the human image of the thing
    in the heart's last blood
            you shine
    as there are stars
    that flicker like human hazards
            through foggy nights.

C   *He was what he could be*

B   For the Dionysus you might have been
    I read you to destruction
    in the grids of everlasting hell.

C   *Burn O dead man burn*

T   Phoenicians
    sailors from Tyre
    ghosts of ships that haunt these ports . . .

Q   *Not one more? One last?*

C   O terrible!
                    Consumer! Day star! Purifier!

> Charger of the flame
> from the hilltop pawing the cliffs
> Destroyer! Builder! Zagreus
> of the spirit
> > of the flesh
> of this human
> > of this heap
> O Nameless! for the flamed . . .

T He floats among the seasons of no tides.
He will not rise. His being
lifts a tide that sings
> *O lost!*
its own requiem
> sweeping in one undying crest
the elegy's endless wave.

Among the Revelations

An apocalypse unrolled between the elements
a voice of burial soft as leaves
floating a forest of heavens in autumn
above the trees and the clouds and the wind-tossing:
It spoke with ease
knowing any word holds the truth.

But the voices had departed
and the waters rolled above the trees.

For the many
just that remains
of which your christ is oblivious
and just that escapes
that makes his dream.

So your acts of revelations
are like an ocean in an empty shell
and your religions
oil in a wound
you are bound to tear open
but to fail along the edges
allows the moment that discloses
what it is that moves
among the rising to no ends.

It wings among the waves.
It spins among the furthest things
in the mornings in the bushes
three star lengths away.

Only so
        I move among the pieces
among the sanies
        where the clarities abound
in the puddle of the carrion
below the rock
        the white roots of it
edging through the grain.

A dead clump of rushes
a down of pondweeds
a sink of life killing life

and from the gases
the cells the sea weed
planorobis among the snails
charon of the whirligigs
Saprini Sarcophagi
the master ghouls
all workers in putrefaction

the white bark of them egg-laying
a white manna of the sea.

Between the sea-lives and the land
the freezes and the thaws
for feather-stars and for us
of feldspar and quartz
silicas and phosphates
the lichen that grows everywhere
of the sea cows and the whales
of the twenty-fourth of the placentals
this one
      O Orpheus of the pines?

INDEX

    Though complete in itself, this elegy is part of an unfinished work in several volumes, Reality Prime. *Such a work, where any page is a note to another, sets up its own system of reference. I am printing below the program furnished for the composition of the music to the Lawrence section. It is intended as an index to point out what is about this elegy, rather than what this elegy is about. —W.L.*

GENERAL

    Reality Prime attempts a cosmogony of poems: on the one hand, how poems ought to be, on the other, how they are not; what the world is, against the poem it isn't.

    Book Two (Some Deaths) revives, for one of its themes, the cult of the dead (cf. "the voices.") In the Lawrence section it is expressed through contrast to a fertility cult (Dionysus): continuity of the dead through cult of the living: Dionysian or Orphic cycle of death and rebirth; cycle of seasons: Lawrence (the bull, Orpheus, prophet, priest) as symbol for creative vitality undergoing sacrificial death. Will the living consume and consummate the dead body? How are the dead to live, to rise = how are the living to live and rise?

THEME

Elegy = search for elegy = search for resolution of individual inner drive (toward life, toward death) vs. general outer pressure (toward life, toward death) = how resolve these extremes? the one and the many? Lawrence (poet, creative individual) and the uncreative mass that creates him? concrete reality (the way outer, common things seem) and visions, dreams? (the way outer common things do not seem).

Search for elegy = search for continuity between dead and living = how demarcate between what is creatively alive and creatively dead, now in confusion through lack of creative human acts = extreme contrast between creative, human aspirations (angels) and "acts" of biological continuity (insects).

Problem: how resolve this death; how justify this experience?

Resolution: biology, plants, insects, flies breeding maggots out of sacrificial flesh; not creative human acts.

Disintegration, the extreme negation = the human creation

PART I *(In the Valley of the Corpses)*

Introduction. The voices of the many. Symbol: life frozen in winter marshes. The outer scene symbol for inner experience traversed in elegiac search. Dionysian mysteries, religious ecstasy, dream acted out as reality in the flesh, evoked as symbol for consecration of body to idea. Deadness of the many vs. vitality they lack.

PART II *(In the Valley of the Poet)*

Isolation of the one. Extremes of individual experience searching for harmony. "I was a musk-ox among men." Symbol: Ocean Floor.

Ooze. Insect death and rebirth = Orphic cycle; Orphic wheel.

TRANSITION TO PART III

From "I heard a nightingale among the whales." Common frame of reference warped. State of music, (sea-counterpart to *Waldweben*). Calm interlude of being floating through nature. ("Meaning" = pattern of the whole experience rather than the specific reference.)

PART III *(Among the Luminals)*

Elegiac search = necessity to weld body to idea, resumed. Extremes between one and many; individual dreams and common reality; aspiration and act. Individual mutilates himself as he kills world's otherness. Birth = breaking from historic womb, impossible. Symbols, intense cold, breaking to individual animal and plant life in sea.

PART IV *(The Return)*

"Dion" (Lawrence) half of Dionysius. Human oneness, broken. Lament for pieces. Echoes of lost Dionysian oneness. Lawrence divided for human consumption. Oneness in death, for Lawrence; disintegration in living, for living.

PART V *(Among the Revelations)*

Exhaustive search; disintegration; experience (as function of biological idea); instantaneous revelation, when time "stops" and the Orphic wheel is broken: purpose. Symbols, the heavens, the maggots. Disintegrated pieces reassembled to divide again. Glorification of maggots, life out of death. World as organism Objective immortality as experience. Lawrence's dead body as food for natural process. The extreme experience evokes the extreme humility. "Catharsis." Biological continuity = Jesus among the maggots; Lawrence among the beetles; Orpheus among the corpuscles.

The Lawrence Section in Relation to Plot of Book Two
(Some Deaths)

Lawrence (d. 1930) is preceded by Apollinaire (d. 1918): The death that follows is communal, The Black Death. The evolution of the one into the many. Individual, unable to die creative death, ceases to exist; biological mass continues.

The Suicide

Dedication: *The Suicide* is in memory of a poet who drowned himself. His skull recounts the three levels of experience he remembered the three times he rose: a bundle of fears; a rock of faith; an anemia of reason. In the culminative wave, the skull tells of a plague that was lifted into the suicide's memory along with the death of his old self. A dirge unites it to statistics.

The book, while complete in itself, is from an unfinished work, *Some Deaths* (Apollinaire, 1930; *Elegy in Memory of D. H. Lawrence*, 1932.) —W.L.

THE SKULL

The skull sea-washed sprouts anemones
where the black mould eats into the bone.
I saw it down the bottoms
among the tails fins scales
of rise and wash of endless days at sea.
Through the petals of the sockets
I saw the buds breathe
like Aeolius among the skulls.
      I heard it
through sponges and brittle stars
polyps and the marine humus:

> *three agonies drowned*
> *and the ninth wave goes to the moon*

Who knows history O foot that walks
      this night of waves
not winged like a messenger
but shoe-hungry like a jew
out of the sea-wombs out of the sea-dead
out of the endless crochet:

FIRST RISING

The birds of the Old Man dove into the sea
to bring the earth to land and make warriors from the mud.

On the mountain top Yellow Crow hacked his finger joint
                    crying
Give me long life and a horse Old Man. Make me a chief.
In the forest with teeth and breasts of iron
Baba Yaga devours the children.

These your bones and you my flesh.
You will never see yourself more clearly.
The angel of death is immeasurable in height
and the space between his eyes is a journey of
                    seventy thousand days.

They have not paid for my flints.
I am done hunting with Odin God of the Wind.
Try these leaves of the sweet flag. They drive away
                    demons.
If dogs eat the after-birth of mares they go mad.

                    And agate is good for fever.
See where my skull was burst to let out demons. I am
                    full of ancient death.
I changed my head a hundred times.
I have slain the sabre-toothed
                    and danced for harvests.
When my flocks were stricken and no lambs born
I rose on an eagle's back into the skies
        to find the herb of life.
My villages sleep at the bottoms of lakes.
The grain over me is billowing and I am coloured with
                    anemones.
And now they rob me of my flints.

I read your coming in a sheep's liver.
           Millions strong your children.
You will sell yourselves to slavery.
I am a Grimaldi with a cargo of flints.
I saw the gold glitter in the graves
and listened to the mysteries of the fathers.
When I died the fall of a twig pointed to the murderer.
I have been burned with axes and with oxen
and my muga set free. I have seen the white dove fly.
Now you rob my grave and leave no flints.

           How shall I hunt
red ochre and gold for corpses?
           How shall I die
without a dog's head
to lead me from the grave?

           The doves of Taravelzita say Kuturung
           Where the talagoya is roasted and eaten there blew a wind
           Where the memmina is roasted and eaten there blew a wind
           Where the deer is roasted and eaten there blew a wind

All are seasons
only spring is an instant
the dead drink from the lake of memory.

Out of the skull
           Orpheus
rose with the fruit of the earth
drank the lips of the dead
called the new-born from the sea

the white clay men sniffed the honeyed wine
tearing deer and the hill goat
leapt to Evoë   tossed the reed wand.

We danced over the new-born
blood-wrought in the wood of the vine
the wild white women dark in the vines
in the sacred thicket of unfooted shadows.

Orpheus first singer and dancer of beats
rushing bull-foot to the temples
the goat killed   the blood poured
the heifers going to shreds   the fir trees
dripped the churned blood.

Over the hills deep in the dark grass
the yoni in wild skins
the phalli in fox pelts
thighs locked in the wild clutch
creating this skull psukhe Iakhos.

      In a holy madness
the Thracian women tore the bone
drank the blood.

His flesh rides the Hebrus
his skull floats down the bottoms.

We leapt for the full jar
for the heavy fleece
for the fruit for the hives
for cities for ships
for Spring
      Dionysus
among remembered things
      from thy springs
Maieutic   Myth   Mystery   O Night
say one more Orpheus rolls
                noiseless
among the shells wash weeds
bones of endless skulls at sea.

SECOND RISING

Young Stephen talked with the angels
brought a letter from God to the King of France

The bay trees withered in the spring
giving a sign of death.

Thirty thousand children marched to Marseilles
singing: We are for Jerusalem to save the Holy Land.
The voices of the merchants rolled back the waters.

At Marseilles   at Genoa   at Brindisi the birds and the
                                                waves
hold the cries of the children
drowned in the slave ships of Marseilles.

In Alexandria the gutters and the docks
hold the voices of the children the merchants sold.

The wheat in France
ripens on the old men
that sold their children into death.

                    my son my son Absalom

These are the children
out of that land

this life of the flesh
this blood
            Zadok and Shalum
and Hilkiah begat and Giovanni begat

this skull
            free
of the fear of death

this marrow brain
nervous axes   spinal flange
flank   face became a name

Bruno

    Mother
Mother   of   God
              of me

from the slopes of Mount Cicala
that rise above Nola

out of Rome   out of Paris
from the Rectors   the Princes

to the sea clusters
to the lime stream

skull-driven for a word.

From the walls of the prison
of the Tower of Nona

from the prayers of the righteous
the lips did not kiss

in the year of Jubilee
in the early morning
to the chanting of litanies
and the songs of the first birds

                  Bruno

stripped by the Servants of Justice
bound to a stake
for a word.

How many years
are eight years
of a Roman dungeon
of the racks of the righteous
of the centuries of doubts
to burn

>   *to bring back what is divine in me*
>   *to that which is divine in the universe*

eyes crackling
            arms blackening

for drums and cheers
    hold fast Bruno
from what inaudible voice?

>   *You who sentence me are in greater fear*
>   *than I who am condemned*

out of the brain cap   out of the earth belly
out of the heaven palate

    burnt alive wind

                out of the spinal marrow
out of the soul worm
this freedom
you might have made a dogma
and saved what mystery
of how many billions?

for the sea fans   for the sea pens

> *who is more deeply moved by the thought*
> *of some other thing does not feel*
> *the pangs of death*

ashes to wind
and the outer wind
gains the essence.

So in the skull he burns
a three hundred year near not-distant torch
(in the early morning the Brothers of Pity
walked him to the Field of Flowers
in the early morning they burned him).

burnt alive
wind
burnt alive.

THIRD RISING

> *It is like the wind*
> *   felt without feeling heard without hearing*
> *It is in the rustle of the leaves*
> *fulfilling the prophecy of the bays*
> *when it plays it is a whirlwind.*
> *One of skull's other world*

Spring came to Black Duck   Battle Creek   Winnebago.
Mississippi bottoms went gummy with new mud.
Wind took the early grass
in Demopolis Alabama.

What roots got sap
buried
in the coal fields in Herrin
with the electrodes in Vanzetti?

What song of Orion won
goes out among the radios?

farm decaying   taxes biting
blighted crop digging
ruts in the skull.

Down streets of symbols train
hurrying skulls to further catacombs
endless bodies furnishing endless rooms.

Touched the clothes felt the bone.

An old story
             of death
a habit
        a black suit my father left me.

But we lived. The cord and womb of something
          moving
westward   eastward   toward the stars   toward the stores
through evenings soft with darkening
sun at noon
the odour of the lighter air

the thousand human faces
skeletons of the world
miracles of surgery
rattling fevers in a wind.

Fled the cracked chatter
of the skull's thousand selves
for a plague of wars   hungers   states   laws

the temples   the towers
sinking into darkness
like an ocean after drowning.

I heard it
out of rocks   days rivers   human
eyes   hands   faces

along the river in the river lights
watching footsteps   leaning over shoulders
in the voices of the children

                Go blind.
                Refuse thoughts   hopes   despairs.
                Blot out old words the body breaks.

                Above the paves
                the flesh harpoons
                the Arctic blood

                and spring
                        a whale
                spouting one white tree.

Down streets of passengers
charging the fortress I was battling

Tristan's features in repose
going to hell at a dozen different tables
                in a chew of bread

losing a hundred instantaneous Isoldes
whose beauty cracked into a gesture
                as they passed.

The word   the look
the adding silence   the unspoken partings
where the spirit flies and the shoes stand still
the indomitable presence of a habit
draining out like sand through one's fingers.

Down the windows of the shining stores
heard the voices

>   Pound the glass.
>   Say the world is full of diamonds
>   only it is your irises cut to strips.

>   *The tree then has grown an inch*
>   *no one measures*

Found no comfort for this
but the touch of bark
gnarled with years
freshening darkly under rain.

And the voices
mortal and immortal
sounding as if tragedy were a bell

someone else's
tragedy appropriated
a persistent tragedy of relations.
And not

The hour struck. I leapt.
Down the sea-wall   bell on bell
mounted on reverberation.
The body rose   the body sank

reeled against the rivers of the graves.
The last insulation reaching
a cohesion of deafness of blindness.
I say it
fathoms   centuries   days
from the waters
in the tables of the seasons
in the numbers of the suicides.

> *Builder*
> *for thy sins I have suffered*
> *and for mine in making you*
> *and in that*
>> *no salvation*

Here I hung
on the spearpoint of an expectation

blind like a crystal
but amorphous like a sense
of blindness and the illusion
of stars falling into place.

Moved through flowers on a hill
where trees and grass and earth
took off from humans human smell
and gave them theirs.

Heard the wool of white sheep thickening
the sound of grass growing   the sun
rising with those early stars
that were with it when being
first moved these lovely things.

Swept through all the sciences
to bring home living in one mystery
a poem no one knows.

It walks talks moves sings
in the shadow of each thought
of the nervous twitches of each brain
oscillating from suicide to suicide.

Here any word holds the truth

a face in the dark
a body in the sand
a grove of wheat tree tall in fall
          moving in the wind
prairie drying dust in a dry wind

a page of worlds
ruled with streets   rivers   margins of lakes
quiet in the wheat-dark glow of Wanakanda
          now all
within the margin of the skull

                    heard it count the waters drop by drop

Saw the buildings rise and fall
new towers toward the heavens.
Saw the towers fall.
Saw the towers rise.

Saw the further children sailing
further from a new Marseilles

to the drying of the sea
and the ships cracking

the ghosts of further children
flying further from a new Marseilles.

Saw the earth as python
                swallowing whole
the shoes and buttons coming out
neatly wrapped in excrement.

Then a loop the loop back
and death moved on
and I went downward.

O merchandise of endless ends
among the orders from Cedar Rapids

among the stuffs from Milan and gold wrought in the north
among the white dwarfs   among the suns
what song of Orion won
goes out among the radios?

I etherized the thing
frayed only inwardly
in a continual rocking of despair.

Lived lies
told tales
visited graves

lay at midnight in her arms
too close together
ever to be a grave apart.

How many nights we talked our love
in a dry perversity of words
        that said like Jesus
nothing?

Goddess ever-rising sea-clipped from the wave
sing for Adonis coming and coming to you
at such and such a rate
or leave it

Here's for Cactuses.
For roots and tides to track us down.
Forget your grubs that trellis eyes
and flake your hands to honey with the bees.
Say good-bye to death.
Ride out this wash of wombs
below the skull below the sea.

      O race   my race
where is a song
soft as wool to wrap your heart in
and let you ravel and beat against the threads?

Regard and guard this skull.
Say it sang. Would you treasure it more
among a thousand unsinging skulls?

What capacity for work
for an apparatus made for song.
R. I. P. R. I. P.

O woods and wilds
                wilds of the wood
wild woods
        and skies
sing of lost sounds and worlds.

And monuments melt.
Go blind stars.
Let nights darken
and sing.

Or leave it

close to silence as it has been
on the bottoms of the sea-floor
this plain-song of a pearl
that holds the fractures of a world

to return to you
O wax among the seas
encrusted like an oyster
annointed with barnacles
whisked among the orifices
in a wild lament of moons.

Quetzalli   Phœnix of the Aztecs
Trumpeter of Guinea   Builder   Father of the Rocks
Cordillera of the mountains

          to the last dog and back
these teeth against death

          always that inch from your eternities.

All my words
ring the skull with moons
grind like a noisy pebble
the sweetly running ball-bearing universe
noiseless in the silence of god's holiest oil.

Our honesty breaks us
leaves no singing but our night

                    past the globigerina
                    down the last bottoms
                    the skull gleams

Turn a page.
Turn up new roads and winds and days
and turn another page

>*Marry with the daughter of the wind*
>*Wave on the sea-floor*
>*Be a sea-anemone*
>*rooted in hermaphroditic rock.*

When the world goes voodoo
and the dog-gods win
give my last bone to a down-growing root.

When the skulls of all of us
rattle at kingdom come
save that bone:

The people of Massachusetts have a date with god.

Give it a witch doctor.
Bury it in a swamp.
Beat on its grave rain-dogs.
The skull pounds   beats   kills

the flesh breaks   the heart breaks   the bone breaks
and the soul breaks.

You will find it where the squares are marked
luminous white dice each
incandescent like a skull.

THE NINTH WAVE

Say one more skull
leaves the sea-bottoms leaves the sea-floors
hangs above the voices winds pulses trees

what it is he wins and loses
among the rising and sinking without return.

Skull among the stars and on the sand
singing to the wind and to the dead
remembering in the rise and fall

> No more the burial with flints.
> No more the white bird . . .

body blackening
> flesh cracking

wind spreading
Black Death.

Who'll run with urine
to ask advice of a Jew?
All are dead
> for poisoning wells

for spreading basilisk juice in egg shells.

It is in the wind
> planting death on trees

to make all growing things
everlasting epitaphs.

It is in the skull
never mad enough for this marriage

but in the hour
among beds bells   rocks   fields   suns
it carries in the bone
to its last kiss of waves:

THE NINTH WAVE

Black Death

These were the warriors
blue-eyed from the north
in bear skins and wild boars'
chariots and the javelins
shaggy-haired   the wild cries

> *the crow screams*
> *Pharomel! Pharomel*
> *sing of the blood.*

These were the signs:
houses full of the wind
vineyards crumbling
            owls and grass
mounting the capitals

            cold wind of 900s
            waiting the thousandth

roads broken and the raids
from the north   from the east

> *Pharomel that fought with the sword*

trees bled   shoots ripped from the bark
stars revolved   the dog-wood went white
and the red trees blossomed over the bones
the 1000th spring.

Arms clanged on the fires   the women wove
seed was planted and the fields turned.
From the land again the fires and the hearth
beginning again in the fathers and mothers

houses of virgin wood and the castles
following the colds winds and the 900s

the temples rising out of the soil
buttresses flying and the spires mounting.
Crusades and crusaders   Crécy and the battles
the dead of Beziers
the butchered   the burnt and "God knoweth his own."
the jousting   the victories   St. Louis and Egypt
stakes and the cross and the heretics flayed
banners and the cross and the sign of the lamb
the shrieks of the tortured cursing the abbeys.

      Then the pest.
The Brandenburg men sprouting heads on buttocks
Satan in Aquarius   a comet in the Ram
eclipses in blood
stinking mists   rains of snakes
storms   floods   locusts knee-high
dripping the signs

        Aye
and   all   the   people   died

    In the cinnamon and ginger

in the pepper and cloves
from Arabia   from India
in the camphor and tragacanth
mastic and balm
from Persia and Ceylon
in the sugar and the dyes
the scents and the gums
in the indigo and alum
the ivory and the pearls
in the caravans from China
the rats carrying fleas
the Black Death.

From Marseilles and the rivers   Alexandria and the ports
along the roads quick through the trees
flailing the land with the millions of dead

Black Death the seed grain of the soil
ground into soil   milling out flowers
out of the stones   death and the petals
stemming   raining out of the red
blood through the soil
                              boils and bells
chorals of chimes for the Black Death.

Scothus walking the waves to Britain
swearing the sea was a holy field
plucking vermillions to throw at the Bishop.

Plague infected the seed of the land
Cities shrank   pastures dried
the crops deserted and the roads
sinks of infection

            was the fruit of the 1000th spring
rivers of blood heavy with corpses

each hermetic ghost
sealed in a sheet of words
mumbling to himself
the endless monologue of being alive

      So the spirit dies
      but the flesh survives

We the chosen spotless as the sun
wretched we sang Stabat Mater Dolorosa
we the Bianchi white in linen
holding the whips and the three-tailed scourges
between the banners   the spiral candles
between the shoulders   the congealing blood
the fingers cut to make god live
that he may lift the plague from us

      The waters closed over the darkness.
      Under the waves
      drowned ladies
      floated their draperies.
      I rose into death
      bursting like a chrysalis
      long tapers of light.

free from stain
arise and do not sin again
that god may lift the pest from us

      struck the shoulder beat for the blood
      washer of sins and the Black Death millions

      a metamorphosis?
      the tubular termites?

      ant fodder to the fore

a dial twist to the left

what horde my god my lord
oral to stercoral
brackish dill they swill

the darkness rolls
over the hovels
three fathoms deep

the Enormous Ma
mills them like pods

puppets sing
        busy   busy
larvae suckle
nymphs rehearse

        in the beginning
        in the beginning

Away fly
turn up another page and turn and fly
Skeletons of the world
                        reporters of plague
raking the pest through the grain

one wave length from a myth
                                one
dial twist from a story of kings

Our fingers touched: heard a siren sing of

centuries of seasons
buzzing of bees   caterpillars gnawing leaves
snowy fortresses of trees

spring sea churning curds

earth seeding into breathing plants
thighs with thighs
fingers gripping in a flight of spasms

dreaming what you might have been
singing dying to a lover's death

the darkened taxi cleaving
the heavy haze   the night   the spring

heard a siren:
                linguals will explain
everything but this

What in one split second
have we touched

R. I. P.   R. I. P.

There the leathery lips rotten with suffering
gnawing at famine   tearing the corpses
the hearts corroding scourging the flesh
to the sound of the whips tanning taint and infection.

                Side by side
                we talked and moved
                                reading
                rows of roads and the rose
                choked with suicide
                                reading

                stocks are moving states are building
                        and the skull is moving

fleeing the pest
flooding the fields with the Black Death millions

down the drains   along the bottoms
the children   the unborn
the dead births
    all meeting all
in the sea
        in the rivers
in the waters of the skull.

She bedded to Jesus drank Mary's blood
another blossom out of Tuscany
Saint of Sienna plaguer of sins
showing the Pope the road to Rome.

      I saw my end. In a chamber alone
      they shut me up. When they heard the cries
      they broke the door. They found me
      tearing my entrails. Then I confessed
      and died in the faith. See my hand
      the black stain from his thumb

grave diggers trenching corpses swelling
a Lazarus of boils rising from the skull

outward flew the winged spirit of light.

    Orpheus Eubios Mother
   your son is marvelously sick
   He has fire in the heart
   Tell Sister Louda and Olga
   he doesn't know where to go

   Mother the fire the words scorch

Mother Mother

from time   from time
burn juniper shrubs and berries
fumigate death O cypresses and pines
clean the land beech and aloe
balm and mint   rosemary and thyme
clean corruption green rue
amber mastic   laudanum   storax

> *sexless in this bone blood skull*
> *strung from the beams*
> *but no Christ*

Rode with Diana   danced with the whippers
          raced the pest
with mothers   with sons   lovers
          flying
Black Death

> *I escaped but they followed*
> *They found me at night and took me*
> *60 miles off the coast of Boston.*
>
> *On the beach they built a fire.*
> *I was one quarter consumed before I could*
>   *speak.*
> *I said*
>   *we met at night in a dream*
> *You are mad too but trained to quiet*
>   *I know the world*
> *further than the beach combers . . .*

CLOSE

His skull rolls down the bottoms
consumed not by Thracian women.
The black rot eats into the bone.
      I saw it
like an anatomy in the sea-roots
      flowering from his eyes.

When the wind blows it sings:

Structure is the soul's skeleton. Over its mould
bone flowered into stone and his dream built
a vista of towers.

To the last dog and back
till the dreamless flesh dissolved
and the dream slips
through the skull's hollows.

Out of rocks days rivers roots
      the mammal egg

out of the ovum bed
      the vaginal stretch

out of the bursting follicle
      the fœtal skull

fathoms deep the globigerina
crushes into the sockets.

Mother that bore me
      time O tide

for the ectoderms
        the cœlentrates

for the hollows of the tissues
        the nervous twitches of the brain

for the skull
        the sea-fans   the buds of cells

the rain of dead things
drop on the sea-bottom
their eternal floor.

The darkness closes
on a gleam
a deep sea fin discloses

        out of the blood
the turquoise shell

        out of the brain stem
the phosphorescent skull.

        fathoms deep
the stalks   gills   filaments
of rise and wash of endless days at sea
open the heart valves
drink the lips of the dead.

Creep into the sockets, wind
Come down into the skull
Old Man of the Sea.

The chart is the destiny of the year
        column for column
                one side for one side

by the names of the months
        by the numbers of the suicides.

Not in fall nor winter but in spring
the record grows
        the numbers mount
                to meet the longer season.

It follows the older years
        the days lengthening   the figures rising.

No more for these
        nor him
                but numbers

dead to suffering
immortal in statistics.

Spring is the season
        fulfilling the coroner's wisdom
                fattening prophetic numbers
                        of the older years and older seasons.

Black buds push from the trees
the rivers bulge   the charts receive
the live numbers
                        into the lime salts
the bone spores   running
gathered to the rows and columns
from the mountains and the flats
from the sea-nodules   from the shell ooze
floating to the sea-bottoms in the waters of the night

to the marine socket   to the brine pap
the empty rooms deserted of tortures
gone   open to sun and to spring
in the waters of the skull
in the darkness of the numbers.

Steel 1937

Out of the earth belly   out of the heaven strain
out of the blood   the steel ores
out of the earth mother   the iron
fathered by a pick axe and a man.

Back in the year one the ice moved and the dry times came and the
     flood poured.
Lightning struck the trees and the coal came.
And a light struck someone's head with a dream of steel.
And it came.   Up on the iron range
the mines give up their stuff in little cars.
In upper Minnesota and Michigan
the men go down and pick
eight hours a day   come up after every shift
to walk home with lamps on their hats and black in their pores
of what the steel came to be.

Out of the earth belly   the iron ores
out of the earth skull   the bellows and the spades
out of the limestone   out of the coke
out of the blast furnaces
in the beginning   the fire came.
Prometheus the Greeks called it
out of the ashes of the fire on a rock
the iron came.   Someone saw it
and the steel began.

What is it?   Description of the thing?
the books give it and the blood knows it
and the little life it gives
is exactly what we take.

Go back to the year one or any time.
Go down to the earth bottoms now.
A thousand feet under the rafters
where the coal and iron lie   and the men. Scratch it and you'll find
a geography of lies.

Go back through the centuries the skull holds.
Go down to the mines.   Out of the earth belly
out of the world maw   there's a story that burns
like iron into steel in the blood of all the women and the men
to burst all human and inhuman laws
that hold them in and starve them and break them
and kill them again and again.
And they will not be held in.

All the complications of our lives and days
confusions of cash and love and sweating centuries of things done and
        undone
stones we left behind in Egypt or Peru
of days we danced for stars   for suns   or loved   or were alone
hacked our fingers to make the blood come true
all the stories of all the days since Abraham
fold and unfold   mix blood with blood and both with all the life and
        blood that steel compounds
in a parallelogram of cells and a prism of forms
that lights up from the mine bottoms up
a steel of the blood
and we call it the human name.

Alcoa

I don't want to know the name of this town.
I don't want to know the reasons why
it spells two more dead.
But still I know.   From the earth
in Alcoa   from the corpses   gas   guns
from the pictures Mellon buys and gives away
from the dividends that mix with the dead
the aluminum smells bad.
The coffee pot spells death.

　　Who draws the line at Alcoa?
　　Who's the Rembrandt of the law?
　　We'll find out in the dirt roads
　　and shacks of Alcoa
　　who draws the dividends and the corpses
　　out of a little less pay.
　　Is there a painting a man can crawl in
　　and call his own?   streets?
　　a lodge?   the A. F. of L.?
　　or an aluminum bullet that comes his way?

Is this canvass
signed Mellon   to death
County of Blount
State of Tennessee?

Who says the sun slants like hot aluminum today?
and the food cooked brown
and the supper tonight
salted with two more dead
at a little less pay?

They buy the El Greco that Mellon buys
who give it a blood bath
that each picture knows
death to death as El Greco painted it
three hundred years ago.

Who wins slower than bullets and death
but we who smell the death of our own
like a beetle miles away
and will not   no never
to death and deaths call it a day
or anything but our death
to live for
as they lie dead for
life in Alcoa
miles away.

Steel

What is it?   A commodity?
an object of exchange?   a process for reducing
the building of people and of things
to balances in the bank and sweat and blood?
Out of the earth belly   out of the September womb
crisis in embryo   murderer of bodies
exploder of dreams we put together again.
Steel file that rasps against the bodies
gnaws us to hungry teeth
walking stomachs of the time
swollen bellies flopping against the steel walls that hold us in.
And if it weren't steel what would it be?
We call it steel   cell block of the world
    prisoners of the age
    in the prison of the age
    and we measure all the freedom of our time.
But in our hands elsewhere and in our heads
it is a different thing
and we say the world shines tomorrow like steel in the sun.

Steel

Steel was something else once in someone's head
a dream and a vision of things to be
and it came.   Out of the earth belly
out of the mother ore.   Inanimate you might say.
But there's a dialogue in such stuff
that bursts its laws back in the bone
and they meet.   Not only with shells
that drop from heaven and explode
flesh and bits of steel in Shanghai streets.
Inside   inside the blood   night and day
a battle of carbons goes on
as in each Bessemer the steel men stoke.
The steel bends us or we bend it.
One way or the other
we meet.

In Gettysburg one morning at dawn
I was the first one about and the air was clear.
I walked among the cannon and the graves
and caught a whiff of Pittsburgh coke in the morning air.

I followed it.

Inside this blast furnace the pig iron is poured.
It comes out shining like a rail.
Inside is like the inside of a star.
Such things go on as might make the figure of a man.
And it does.   Carnegie or John Bogovich.
You or me.   Sticks   boats
freight cars from Siam
the movements of many things
moves together as we and the steel meet

Inanimate you might say but the ingots it makes
mould the movement of the body from which it came.
Or we mould it.   One way and the other
we meet

Sometimes the earth shivers.   An earthquake we say.
The rails buckle.   The steel buildings fall.
Sometimes the laws of people and things meet
A revolution we say and solve nothing
by giving it a name.   This moves also with the men
and the death in them and the steel they make.
One way or the other again and again
they meet.

Continual revolution of the blood.
Continual cataclysm of the brain   catharsis of thoughts
things   deeds . . . . . We need to be
the continual animation of a dream
to bend the steel or be bent by it.
A man should live these things as he lies in graves
neither up or down but sideways with his head and feet
pointing to human and more human poles
and the hand touches another and we meet.

The Nightingale
(for D. H. Lawrence)[*]

I heard a nightingale among the whales,
    clean as a shark's tooth among the shoals.
It was singing,
        calling,
among the sea mammals,
        among the ghouls,
the octuples among the souls. . . .

        My brother rests among the butter,
but something on the wing recalls the years
        when it was southeast over Montauk.
There the wind trolls slowly,
    above the reeds,
        among the hills
where the dialect changes with the ridges,
    like Switzerland among the bluebells.

The edelweiss we picked persists among the leaves.
    It is turned to day-by-day
        and yellows slowly.
It spreads its wings
        and folds and unfolds.
Among the bells,
        among the fine frosts.
Ipecac is also a flower that grows;
ipecac is a name above the mountains.

---

[*] In his later poems, Lowenfels occasionally borrowed from earlier work as he clearly did in "The Nightingale." Cf. pp. 46-47 above.

94   Walter Lowenfels

The trellises are made of gold;
    seconds stretch into grills.
Among the butter an hour is worked into a blossom,
    on the one hand golden,
        on the other, an edelweiss, a bluebell
            or an hour.
It goes stitch by stitch by tower —
a poem monumental as a butler.
O children that knit their acts among the butter!

Every Poem Is a Love Poem

I am trying to break through this language to get to
        fireboxes
        Cooper-Bessemer compressors
        magnetic films
without the copperbelt lining that keeps my hope
        from exploding out of this typewriter,
        desk, window, through the pines, down the
        Little Egg Harbor River, across the
        Continental Shelf.
"Reaching for ultimate simulation"
        is an earthborn facility
        where the almost limitless field
           of space and electronic simulation
reproduces the condition of
        roll
          pitch
            yaw
              rotation
                buffeting
all at various controlled speeds
        of three-dimensional vibration.
(Engineers — check your answers and mail today —
        pleasant living conditions
        company stability & prestige
        desirable fringe benefits such as
        year-around recreational facilities, etc.)
and love
    LOVE
     L O V E
   (also more love)
              And yet

what instrument will measure
    on the moon
    on the planets
many minds that work as one
    (such as yours perhaps)
("somewhere you stand waiting for him")?

Through a column to a detector
in the form of burned-off gas
after an electric oven decomposes.
I am finished
        with thrust deflection
        secondary injections
        cryogenics —

I rely only
        on plastic sleeves
        optical comparators
        propulsion systems
        and Slade's elastic bind.
Otherwise I am lost
        (don't stand there waiting for me!)
Missiles are thrusting farther with greater accuracy
"impossible" control jobs are becoming daily routine
when it comes to colonizing the moon —
the regenerative liquid metal cell
will replace
        power steering
                air breathing
                        and
Anyone for Mars?
      to see   to measure   to know?
and to love
      LOVE
        L O V E?

Elegy for the Old Language

Language in the U.S.A. has become so disturbed,
    when a poet uses it for resonance-capture,
      everybody thinks his truth is lying — that makes people
    feel bad and they kill themselves.
In the solar mirror in which we live, the coroner
    thinks it is the poet who has committed suicide . . . .

Motivists speak of our weak character.
    Across the desert border,
    on the Aztec altar where
    we are all lovers in the flesh,
we watch those who escape the cyanide
    having their hearts ripped out.

Even the "earth" in "rare earth" is not completely descriptive.

On the high end of the verbal spectrum
where words are metal, you pour out like beads;
only a poem measures the optimum relationship,
unveiling the riddle of rolling friction in the
                    magnetism of the sun.

Slice light the way you want it.
Where do we go from minus 320°F?
Magnetic exploration along the crystal axis?

Guided tour of the solar system?
Reaching tomorrow is our job;
    success is to survive as a turbulent
    transfer in the cybernetics of cre-
    ation — not a chopped, stabilized amplifier.

On this vertical oscillator radar tracking unit,
    lively as a walk on the moon,
from kitchen to stars,
    camera weds duplicator
    fishing for neutrons.
Cosmic butterfly
    spreading its wings
to absorb the eternal flow of solar energy.

In conclusion, comrade space,
The Big Elk is rounding the Cape of Good Hope.
    The horn is on the deer. Beyond magnetic memory
    bells are sounding in star spaces
    and the Dog mounts the Bear.

Are you ready to go? Do you know which way the
    microwave is moving?
Have you got the ice-cutter ready for the
    passage around Point Vega?
And he named me Antrium and I said: "You don't
    frighten me. I have been used to you for
    ten thousand years. You always tell the last
    tale and you never win the first story.
Cut out the chatter. The time has come to start
    the Big Journey and we are all ready."

Shield for the battle for survival in space;
electroluminescence;
plasma flame spray;
plumbing for posterity.

Jukebox in the Coalfields

It's Rosefield Gardens, Richeyville, teen-age coke bar in this Appalachian coalfield. You dance here or not at all. Unless you are older and go to Bentleyville, and mix on the crowded floor where the Polka Dots are making jive and the admission is 85 cents at the door.

The girls come into the coke bar from the cold night with kerchiefs on their heads. They swish behind a partition and emerge with freshly fluffed hair, to the tunes of **St. Louis Blues** or **Kisses Sweeter than Wine**. And Bill steps off with Hannah, and Ed puts his cigarette aside. What does the jukebox say?

You will hear its song on winter avenues or where the wolves prowl on Rocky Mountain snows. It vibrates in the submerged ninth of icebergs floating down the Atlantic from the Spitzbergen side of the pole.

Drown Bill and Hannah in coke, pour coal dust over them like a shower bath — they will go down once, twice — but the third time you will find them coming up like Venus on a sea shell, singing and swaying away. There is no silence here, and the miners young and old have a language that draws black music from the earth and keeps the world in a singing boil.

It is within giant peripheries that choices of action protrude like stalactites among the icy caverns of the mines. You will not know the coal miner from a word, only in some secret crevice of his blind will-to-be.

Good-Bye, Jargon

(elegy for a small press)

Since 1492 some 175 million of us in the U.S.A. have
    advanced from deserts, wastes, forests and lonesome prairie
to a thruway of cities, highways and missile bases, with
    unemployed men and women on every corner.
There is still one practically uninhabited mountain pass
    and that's the poetry-crossing over the Big Muddy.
Publish a book of poems in the Strontium Age and you can enjoy
    all the rigors of striking out on a new Oregon Trail.
The rapids, the natives, the rain, the heat, the cold, the thunder —
    they're all there — particularly the long lonesome days and
    nights when you don't see a chipmunk reader peering
    across the poetry route along the Columbia River highway of
    your dreams.
When you consider there are 400,000 of us turning out the stuff
    these days, and several hundred of us proclaimed the "Greatest
    Poets of our Generation," you can realize what a huge vacuum
    our non-readers are creating.
Do you wonder the earth is slipping on her axis and the moon is
    a decimal off-center every other thousand years?
    There aren't enough poetry readers turning pages
    to keep the side-slip of our jet travel around the
    universe on an even keel.
We are slipping down the hydrogen side of the galactic spiral
    with poems receding from our unreading eyes, and
    everybody wonders can the next explosion save us from
    smashing our lovely planet without even an elegy for its good-bye.
In the great silence even Tiberius no longer asks what song
    the sirens sang; what the Emperor of Today hears
    is the mushroom screaming:
And that's the song.

Welcome Home to Cubby

Among the sixteen thousand insane inmates, he was the conscious
                                                                maniac.
    He doesn't want to be normal. He can't stand the
    sexless odor of it.
Something happened to him — in the navy — in the army —
    in the Red Hook dives of his Brooklyn underworld.
    The lining of his country's stomach got turned inside out
    for him and he saw what he could not swallow.
Some people say he's nothing but a dirty writer.
    I hear the pin-drop of what he has lost unloading
    its specimen over the Flatbush Avenue marshes.
Of course we can't stand it. It's our personal fall-out
    trickling down the Gulf Stream. It's the crotch
    of our Pentagon's cleanest H-bomb. It's the other
    self we are trying to turn our back on — the corpse
    of the old Dog-Eat-Dog lousing-up Rockefeller
    Plaza years after it should have been laid out.
It's too late now for burial. It has to be cremated.
    Meanwhile, to participate in the ceremony, Cubby
    has himself to burn.
That hiccough laugh he gives as he talks and grabs for his
    anti-allergy pills hasn't to do with anything funny.
    He's allergic to the universe. He's looking for
    everlasting love in the urinals. It's the acid drip
    of human intercourse that's biting him. He is
    working toward that one word that will drop us all
    without an echo of his being alive alongside three
    billion others for whom his desperation is the tombstone
    they have to overturn if they are to survive.

For a Hemiplegic

Lillian is alive, more alive than she was. Also — something has died — a little part of the brain that controls the functions of her left arm and leg has become extinct.

We think of death as a single act: here today, gone tomorrow. There are all kinds; this is one of them. A little death you can recover some life from. . . . The little deaths are not alone — always someone dies with you.

Lillian's spasms of pain as she tries to learn to walk and her leg crumples under her strike me like a seismographic shock registering on needles miles away.

It might be wonderful to be yourself — completely intact and alive. It doesn't happen. The molecules won't have it; the waves are against it. The human grid registers the heartbeat you skip.

I think of Lillian's mind as a lovely lake that mirrors many facets of trees and sky and people. Somehow a stone has fallen into it. It sends ripples over the water of the earth. And none of us are the same.

Whitman spoke of the "divine concrete" — Lillian lives it, very close to the earth. This fact has a series of implications that practically no one but a hemiplegic can realize.

Her down-to-earth-ness begins with her feet. She has always to be conscious that she has two feet on the ground, because only one of them is a foot she controls. The other she manipulates from the hip, via the brace that keeps the foot from turning over. She cannot turn around or take a step or climb a curb or go over a doorsill or get in and out of a car or room without the most careful and conscious navigation.

The ruling word in her life is "balance." She has to strive for balance in all things. If she fails, she falls. THE FALL is the Great Enemy — always threatening to trip her up, to make her clutch, stumble, hit the floor — with the danger of breaking her hip.

The point I am getting at is that through all this Lillian is sensitive to angles of being alive that few of us feel. And yet, the minute she says, "I like to see new faces — that's why I look at TV," or "Yes, let's take a ride, I want to inspect the sunset," I realize that things like faces and sunsets are special for her because she spent a time out there when she didn't see faces or sunsets.

Who hasn't dreamed of being dead and coming back alive? It is one of the recurrent fantasies of religion, or primitive magic. We beat our fists against the closed door of consciousness that is either on one side of the mirror or the other. Lillian has been on both sides and returns to give us an occasional glimpse of how it is.

We all like being with children. But who glows in the ambience of children as Lillian does. She has to put up pictures all over the room — our grand-children; our friends' children.

In the old days, when she was being hounded by the unAmerican Committee, she carried with her what she called her "objectifiers." These are tiny Indian figures a thousand years old, dug up in Mexico. Fingering them while being questioned on the witness stand gave her, she said, a better balance on the relation between herself and the world. The Mexican figurines are on a shelf in our living room. But they have been replaced as "balancers" for Lillian by more living things — children's faces, sunsets, the water of the lake, the falls by the mill.

Lillian might be said to be half out of her skin; often she has to feel around with her right hand to find out where her left hand is. Nothing is taken for granted. Every inch has to be verified all along the way; otherwise she might break her arm underneath her own weight; or she might take a step without her brace and injure her foot, whose lost nerve has brought back a ghost of the prehensile stage.

Along with the Fall, the enemy is the Cold. Nothing to keep the balance of body heat except external aids — electric blanket, woolen throws. On one level, you might say, life has been reduced to an elementary problem: not to fall, not to be cold. And this is extended to a certain childlike simplicity about many things. On certain complicated questions, she will just go silent.

And yet let a deer cross the road, or a sprinkling of snow dot the field outside our window, or a familiar face brighten our doorway, and she comes alive like one of those small, folded Japanese flowers when it is immersed in water.

In the 19th century world, when the USA outlook was for continual progress and the eternal verities, a paralyzed person was a burden. In the 1960's, when the rest of the world begins to outstrip us in vision and performance, Lillian's struggle to be alive gives every face a new look, every day's sunset a different glow. Nothing is the same; all things are different because one tiny centimeter of cortex has died, leaving the rest of her still terribly alive.

> Flowers in the ward
> smell of aspirin, and days
> when I loved you like peonies
> and hyacinths and fields
> of daisies . . . fade out.
> I love you like a hospital,
> like a wheel chair,
> like the hemiplegics
> floating in the pool;
> like the young head nurse
> walkless from polio
> smiling from her chair:
> **your wife**
> **will be walking by herself soon.**

Let's get a bulldozer,
plough up every street we ever lived,
    begin all over from scratch,
as if it were the first day
    we met, and you were lame
but I never noticed
    because you were so much you
and did everything your own way
    anyhow.

Believe me it's not all gloomy,
    like when you're half-paralyzed
and showering is an agony
    on a hard chair.
We can always rely
    on doing it together —
        You hold the shower rail
and I hold you,
    and what love
        can be purer or cleaner
than going into the shower
    hugging each other?
        Just to stand up
and get soaped
    clean to the end,
so happy you don't have to
    wash alone in that cold
hospital chair.
    So, as I said,
        it's not all gloomy —
just a question of balance.
    I love you,
even though all I say is,
    "please pass the soap."

* * *

In the beginning
it was easy
to stretch out
beyond the typewriter
and start yapping
death at the moon.
Now,
the spine of the Andes
under our fingertips,
the last Inca god
kissing Tierra del Fuego,
our sun-song crossing
the Sierra Nevada.
The two of us —
you with your iron brace,
me with my hand in yours —
faithful only
to being alive.

American Voices (2)

Across Jersey sand barrens
night is cradled in the arms of pine branches,
peach blossoms are shaking on the bough.
    A jet plane from Pomona Air Base
zips its star across our sky,
but the ground of liberty is still gained by inches.

> *My name is Larry. My letter appeared in the*
> *Wayne University Collegian, Detroit, Michigan:*
>   "The world is not Americo-centric, and we are
> participants in a world community, not masters
> of it."

    In South Jersey
across the Land of Lenapes
the deer trail is hidden in the cedar swamps,
cranberry pippins edge out of their moss.
    In Bridgeton
a wife longs by her window:

> *Your ring warms my finger but you*
> *have gone to the neighborhood of death.*
> *I am washing the powder from my face*
> *the lipstick from my lips.*
> *When can we both lean by the wind-blown curtains*
> *and see the tears dry on each other's face?*

    In South Jersey
the wild laurel breathes over our tomato patches.
A pine wind dusts our hands and faces —
a farmer turns in his sleep wondering —
    will morning bring radium or rain?

In a room in Vineland
a mother is parting from her son.
She cries but no sound breaks from her voice.
She clutches at him though her arms are still.
Who hears her song:

> *On the gray birches the moon shines cold.*
> *Soon it will be warm in the woods of South Jersey.*
> *When will my son return?*
> *He was always a man of peace*
> *and played baseball in the spring.*

In South Jersey
whippoorwill calls sharpen our ears,
    blueberry bushes wave through the dark
        and peach blossoms send out perfume
to make a peace treaty with spring.

In South Jersey
the sun is marching north
    15 miles a day.
The tips of our scrub oaks are separating
    into pink threads. Swamp magnolias
are crackling with light.
    In Mays Landing
a girl reads her sweetheart's letter . . .

> March, march, march
> separated by 10,000 miles,
> each in our corner.
> The road is so far,
> When shall we meet?
> What is left us
> but wanting to be together?

A copper coin or a stone
outlives any of us.
Only a good name endures.
We are all brothers,
each a branch from the same tree . . .
If I live I shall return,
if I do not,

we shall live in each other
forever.

> *I am Margaret. My letter was in the Free*
> *Press, Detroit, Michigan.*
>> "I will shortly become a mother for the first
>> time, and this more than any single factor dra-
>> matizes to me the need for world peace."

In South Jersey
we do not yearn for the cedars of Lebanon.
At dawn we drink the alarm-clock blues.
At dusk we eat the petals from our days.
We grieve over endless hungry children.
We mark down carefully how much we can endure.
We grind the tractor on the side of the sun,
flick the sky's face with an oakleaf,
order the bridgekeeper at Somers Point —
OPEN UP!

Over Brigantine we look at the sky.
The rainbow we planted has arrived.
Our sunlight is already
bending across the mountain of today.
We are here!

Message from Bert Brecht

And don't think
    art
is that actor over there
    talking
to that other one
    upstage.
He's
    the third one
you don't see
    talking
to that other one
    you can't hear
offstage.

Epitaph for My Punctuation

Not the absurd, not the inconsequential,
    just the comma of being here
        among milk bottles & constellations
in love with our parenthesis of passage
    between Andromeda and Peekskill
where the world's apostrophes collapse
        into the oneness of all ditto marks & galaxies
            including lovers doing the hyphen
along the mountain-folding
    question mark of Palisades Parkway.

R. I. P.

(after François Villon)

Walter died suddenly at 3 A.M.
>of an insufficiency of arterial beats
>>he never bothered writing a poem about.
We often see his kind around the Movement
>swinging between being everything to all people
>>and a stick of gum to his grandchildren.
>>>Just before he shoved off he wrote us his
>>>epitaph:

After you have burned the remains
>and gotten rid of the ashes —
>>(the cheapest way — no
>>>little urn in the Chapel!) —
if you have a moment between drinks and paying bills
>shake your pen over the table
>>or on the floor for me —
a tiny drop of ink
>tomorrow's children
>>will wipe off easily.

Designed by
Samuel Retsov

∽

Text: 10 pt Century Schoolbook
Titles: 16 pt Chantilly

∽

acid-free paper

∽

Printed by
McNaughton & Gunn